This Book Belongs To

DRAW YOUR BIG IDEA

The Ultimate Creativity Tool
for Turning Thoughts Into Action
and Dreams Into Reality

NORA HERTING
HEATHER WILLEMS

CHRONICLE BOOKS
SAN FRANCISCO

Library of Congress Cataloging-in-Publication Data available.

ISBN: 978-1-4521-5292-9

Manufactured in China

Design by Jennifer Tolo Pierce

10 9 8 7 6 5 4 3 2 1

Chronicle Books LLC
680 Second Street
San Francisco, California 94107
www.chroniclebooks.com

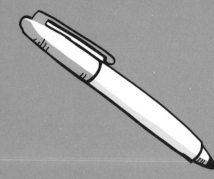

CONTENTS

INTRODUCTION

There are many reasons people find themselves drawing—for creative self-expression, to strengthen an idea, to communicate, to memorialize, or to lead people. We have drawn for these reasons, too, and in the process, we have taught what we know to the business community. Both artistic children, we went to art school, where we met in an art history class. We were alike in our work ethic, our innocent ambition to become professional fine artists, and our desire to help others express their artistic side. (Outside of class, Heather was teaching photography to business professionals through a community art gallery in Minneapolis, while Nora was an art teacher to 500 students on Chicago's South Side.) A few years into school, we were delighted to learn we had each received a full fellowship for teaching undergraduates while we pursued our master's degrees in fine art.

Years later, our backgrounds as artists and art educators brought us to work in a very unlikely place. This place was filled with toys, games, books on business, art, and novels. It wasn't a children's classroom, but a collaboration space run by an international consulting company. Despite the fun atmosphere, real work was done there, but it was done differently. Creativity, collaboration, and action were the fundamental guiding principles.

Here we were trained in the powerful practice of aiding creative work through real-time visual transcription, or what is called graphic recording. Having drawn, up until that point, as an act of creative expression, we now began to experience the power of drawing as a social act, as a way to increase understanding in a group and gain clarity of ideas and purpose. As a new way to facilitate.

We were both attracted to graphic recording because it combined creative expression and collaborative energy. Most important, it fulfilled a real and deep need in the business environment. In 2009 we redirected our efforts from working with the consulting company to focusing on our own visual art—by starting ImageThink.

Now we have trained a full-time team to support meetings and engagements across the globe. We aid the work of huge mergers, corporate reorganizations, innovative directions, and strategies of some of the world's biggest and most respected companies. Our clients have different names for these engagements—strategic planning, ideation, brand visioning, leadership summit—but regardless of the description, they all have one aspect in common: each group faces a problem and is looking for visual help to clarify, communicate, and collaborate in their search for solutions.

YOUR TURN

Now we'd like to teach you what we've taught our clients: how to use drawing to develop thoughts and ideas until you have a cohesive vision you can act upon.

This process begins with taking stock, by visualizing your strengths, picturing your dreams, and exploring what excites you. You will identify a passion and envision your idea as it will exist in the world. This idea might be an online store, an art gallery, a community space, a sign-painting business, a music festival, a coffee shop, a personal shopping service, or a political movement. While these may seem like very different pursuits, they are similar in how they each produce or offer something to constituents who rely on the service or product. Getting to the point where your idea exists in the world takes purpose, a message, and a plan. Let's call it your endeavor.

Regardless of your endeavor's form or financial model, you will need to inventory your resources, clarify your purpose, identify your future customers or users, create a message, and set goals for the future. We have designed the exercises in this book to help you find answers and create a clear plan.

You are embarking on an endeavor that is fueled by your passion and supported by the strengths and assets you already have. In the pages of this book, we will guide you through the processes of self-reflection, articulating purpose, envisioning your new business, and mapping the path to the realization of your endeavor. You will get there by drawing your answers to prompts in exercises that build on one another.

This isn't a typical business advice book. There are enough of those. (We know, because we keep reading them!) The truth is, creating something is not as easy as following advice. The big, important answers aren't in a book. They're inside you. You know yourself best, so you are your own best advisor. We can't give you the answers, but we will provide you with a thoughtful, logical process designed to press your creative buttons, unpack your thinking, and guide you to action.

THE CASE FOR VISUAL THINKING AND MODELING

What neurologists, artists, and designers know can work for you, too. Why do creatives turn to sketching during the ideation phase of a project? It is a quick way to articulate a concept and it stimulates cross-cognitive brain function. In other words, drawing out your ideas leads to a deeper understanding of a problem and faster decision-making.

Contrary to the popular notion that creativity originates in the right side of the brain, visual thinking activates the entire brain. By stimulating the whole mind, you are processing information both analytically and aesthetically in unison. When you draw, or even imagine a drawing in your mind, your prefrontal cortex is activated. This is important because the prefrontal cortex is considered the "CEO" of the brain. In this book you are going to put that CEO to work.

Because we are wired to perceive the world visually, mapping ideas spatially allows multiple concepts to exist simultaneously. It uses our spatial minds to create associations, hierarchies, and relationships between thoughts in a way that linear language cannot. In the end, you are not just documenting information but creating a map that reveals the interconnection between concepts for more holistic thinking.

Drawing provides you with a symbolic visual of your goal and can motivate you in a way that simple text cannot. Once you commit that visual to paper, you are invested in a small but powerful way, because you have put your idea out into the world. Henry David Thoreau said, "The secret of achievement is to hold a picture of a successful outcome in the mind." Athletes and sports psychologists agree that visualization is a key component in realizing success.

YOU SHOULD AND CAN DRAW

This book is designed to allow you to do as little or as much drawing as you would like. Many of the exercises provide you with a visual framework. If you are not inspired to answer in pictures, you can complete the exercises using only words. But we provide plenty of white space for your inner artist and encourage you to complete as many of the prompts as possible with pictures—and here's why:

- Drawing actually comes naturally to all of us. Remember, when you were a child you drew with joy.

- Drawing is a basic communication tool older than civilization itself. Our ancestors drew before they mastered language. The first form of written communication was cave paintings created 30,000 years ago in the Paleolithic era.

- Drawing introduces a sense of playfulness. Approaching challenges with humor and levity will not only help you keep your sanity, it will also aid your creative thinking.

- It's the ideal time to try something new. Undertaking a new endeavor requires courage and a sense of adventure.

- You'll see things differently. Surely this is not the first time you will reflect on yourself, your passion, and your future. But this may be the first time you have mapped, drawn, or diagrammed them. Our process may uncover a new perspective and enable you to remember and better envision your goal.

- Pictures tell a story. Once you have defined your purpose, you will need to communicate it to a variety of people, including your network, future customers, and employees. Having pictures of what you want, the value you bring, and your goal will make this infinitely easier.

CHAPTER 1

PUTTING PEN to PAPER

To get you started, here are some favorite tips that we teach to executives in ImageThink's visual communication workshops. Regardless of how well you think you draw, give these exercises a try. Do the ones that push you past your comfort level. That might mean drawing people, using color, or, if that already comes naturally to you, summarizing big ideas with pictures.

5 *Simple* ⌃DRAWING ELEMENTS

Do you feel daunted by the prospect of drawing? Remember how easy it was when you first learned to draw your shapes. With a little bit of imagination and a few lines, you can transform simple shapes, like these below, into objects you encounter every day.

Stop reading and look around. Yes, now. Choose two objects in your surroundings. Now imagine how they might be reduced to the five shapes you can already draw. Here are some examples.

NOW GIVE IT A TRY!

PRACTICE HERE

fear no STICKMAN (OR LADY!!)

Pictures are powerful, but visuals of people have the most impact. The good news is they are easier to draw than you think. Here is one of our down-and-dirty methods to bulk up your average stick figure.

Write the capital "A" and make it really tall. Now, do it again but add an oval on the top. VOILÀ! You have a head.

Add some appendages. Hands can be mittens or the letter "v."

Simple lines give your stick figure clothing. If both lines of the feet are pointing in the same direction, your stick figure will look like she's walking.

Arrows can help draw attention, imply cause and effect, show sequence, and indicate action. Arrows come in many styles.

arrows

Start with a basic triangle and add a line or rectangle for a tail. Get creative and make that tail curvy, or even swoopy, to make more eye-catching arrows.

PRACTICE HERE

CONTAINERS

ORGANIZE

Containers are simply shapes that hold words. A classic example is a thought bubble.

GIVE CONTEXT

CREATE CATEGORIES

ADD VISUAL INTEREST

So many shapes and figures can be containers.

COLOR

Using color isn't just for aesthetics. We use color to enhance meaning and clarity. Color is a useful tool for . . .

 Highlighting important points.

 Differentiating ideas, themes, and attributes.

 Organizing content for clarity.

PRACTICE HERE

PRACTICE more here...

BRING IT ALL TOGETHER

Exercise the skills you gained in this chapter
related to figures, containers, arrows, and color by
completing one of the following three prompts:

a) Create a visual biography drawing out your achievements.

b) Sketch out the plot line of the last movie you watched.

c) Visually tell the story of your favorite vacation.

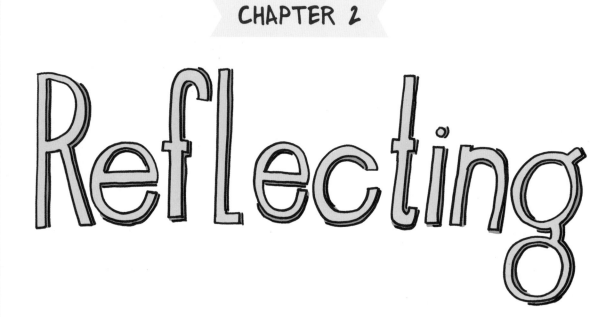

CHAPTER 2

Reflecting

It's time to put your new drawing skills into practice. Completing these exercises will help you reflect on and articulate your strengths, dreams, and joys. In this chapter you will establish where you are today, reflect on past triumphs and fears, and uncover your aspirations and anxieties about the future. You will create an inventory of what you have and what you might need to develop. In doing so, you will take the first step toward identifying and actualizing your dream.

TIME LINE

ON this timeline, record the significant life events—the highs and the lows—that you have experienced. Record them chronologically and align each one with the vertical axis to reflect how they impacted you. Then reflect on the results. What insights did you gain?

What is easy for you?

What is most difficult for you?

REVEAL your VILLAIN

Offer advice to . . .

A Younger YOU

How can you use
this advice now?

TODAY

How far will you go to get
what you want?

Draw the line

Where will you stop?

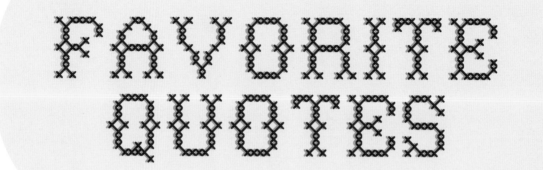

FAVORITE QUOTES

Insert inspiration here!

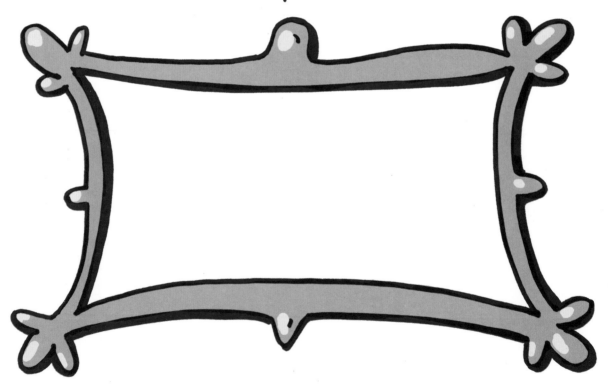

YOUR FEARS

What scared you the most at these ages?

AGE 5

AGE 18

AGE 13

NOW

What skills will help you along the way?

IF YOU HAD A SUPERHERO POWER

WHAT WOULD IT BE?

What gives you stability?

How are you presenting yourself
to the world NOW?

How would you
like to present
yourself in the
FUTURE?

The exercises in this chapter will help you identify what motivates you, gives you energy, excites you, and keeps you going. We will ask you to identify what you're good at, what keeps you focused, and what you would willingly do for free. Once you have captured these passions on paper, you can creatively apply them to fuel your entrepreneurial endeavor.

X MARKS THE SPOT

Think of the activities you do. Plot your level of satisfaction and competency at each activity on the axis. Then look at what you have assigned to the lower left quadrant. Avoid these! If you are doing them now, figure out how you can stop doing them (can you delegate or stop altogether?). You might consider taking classes or focusing on improving the items in the lower right quadrant. You enjoy them, but need to improve your mastery. Now, look at the upper right quadrant. You've got skills here and you enjoy using them. THIS IS YOUR SWEET SPOT!

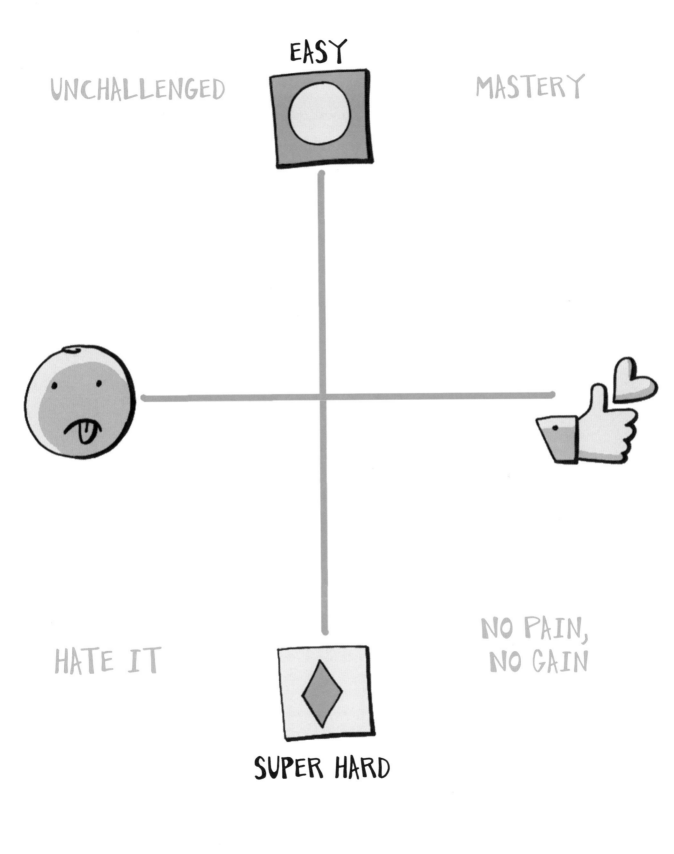

EASY

UNCHALLENGED

MASTERY

HATE IT

NO PAIN,
NO GAIN

SUPER HARD

When are you
intensely focused?

When do you
lose track of time?

What DID you [LOVE TO DO] as a CHILD?

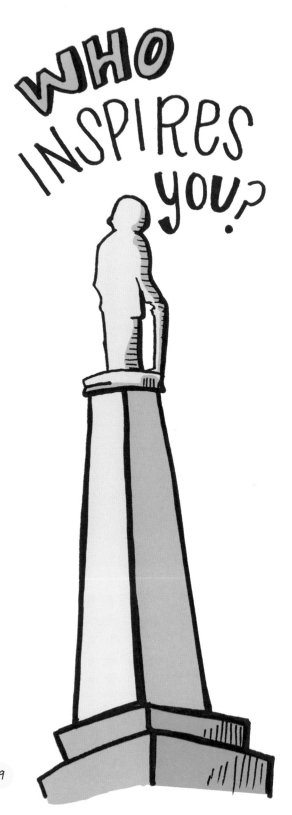

YOUR DREAM JOB

What did you want to be when you grew up? Did it change at different ages? Why? Why not?

AGE 5

AGE 18

AGE 13

NOW

WHAT ACTIVITIES ENERGIZE you ?

Identify three ways you can incorporate
these activities into your day.

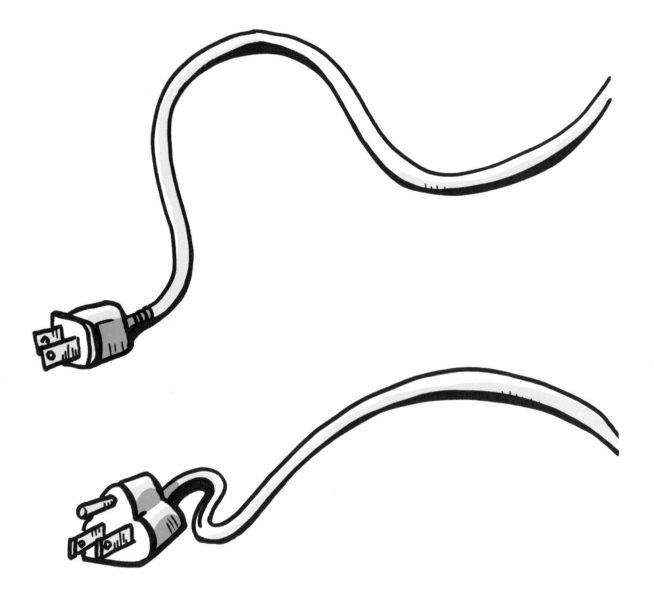

THE Anti-BUCKET list

Your bucket list—which includes all those "must-try" experiences you don't want to miss out on in life—can reveal a lot about you. Make an anti-bucket list which includes those "must-try" experiences that you could gladly miss out on and not regret it. By identifying what you don't need to experience in your lifetime, you free up more time and energy that can be used to focus on the experiences that fill you with excitement. On the opposite page, create your anti-bucket list. We've created our own lists below to help get you started.

NORA'S ANTI-BUCKET LIST

Run a marathon

Read *Harry Potter* books

Make mascarpone

Go to Mount Rushmore

HEATHER'S ANTI-BUCKET LIST

Deep-sea diving

Bungee jumping

Win an Oscar

Learn Latin

What did you learn about yourself in this chapter that will fuel your endeavor?

WHAT PASSION FRUITS WILL YOUR TREE BEAR?

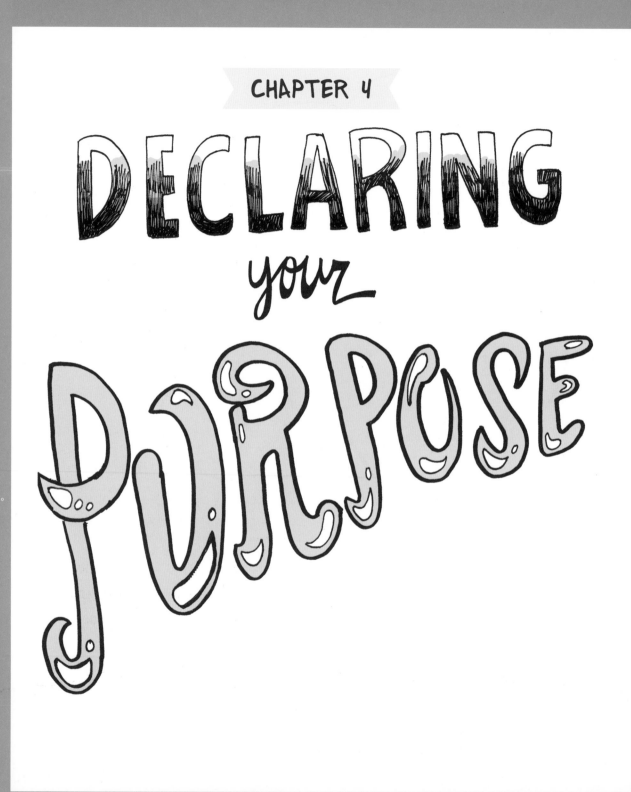

CHAPTER 4

DECLARING your PURPOSE

You have identified what you are good at and what you like to do. Now, ask yourself what is most important to you. The exercises in this section will help you pinpoint your purpose. Your purpose is an internal compass that guides you toward actualizing your dream. In the future, when you are faced with difficult decisions, return to this chapter for direction and guidance.

CORE Beliefs

Identify the things that mean the most to you. These prompts will help get you started.

I believe people are _____.

I am capable of _____.

I accept that _____.

Now imagine what the world would look like if society put each of those core beliefs into practice. What problems in the world would be fixed? How would the world be improved?

When I am 80, I have no doubt that _____.

I trust _____ will _____.

In time, I am convinced _____.

WHAT IS YOUR CREDO?

If you were to turn these core beliefs into simple words to live by, what would they be? Write them here.

72

Circle the top five values that you identify with the most.

INTEGRITY   HELPFULNESS   ADVENTURE

CREATIVITY

OPEN-MINDEDNESS   TRUST   PLAYFULNESS

BALANCE   ALTRUISM

COMMUNITY

NATURE   CONSISTENCY   ORDER

VALUES

HONESTY   GROWTH   OPTIMISM

PASSION   LEADERSHIP

RESOURCEFULNESS   ATHLETICISM

INDEPENDENCE   RELIABILITY   POWER

PRODUCTIVITY   CURIOSITY

HUMOR

EDUCATION   INNOVATION   HEALTH

Don't see one of your values? Write it in!

Take each value that you circled
and turn it into a

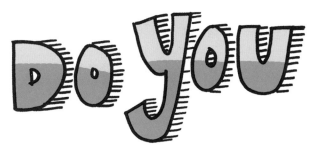

WHAT DO YOU ♥ love TO DO?

List all of your favorite activities—what gets you moving, what relaxes you, what makes you happy to be alive.

In this chapter you identified what you love to do, circled your values, and called out what you believe. That's a lot of work! Now write these items in the empty Venn diagram on the opposite page, as Heather has done in the example below.

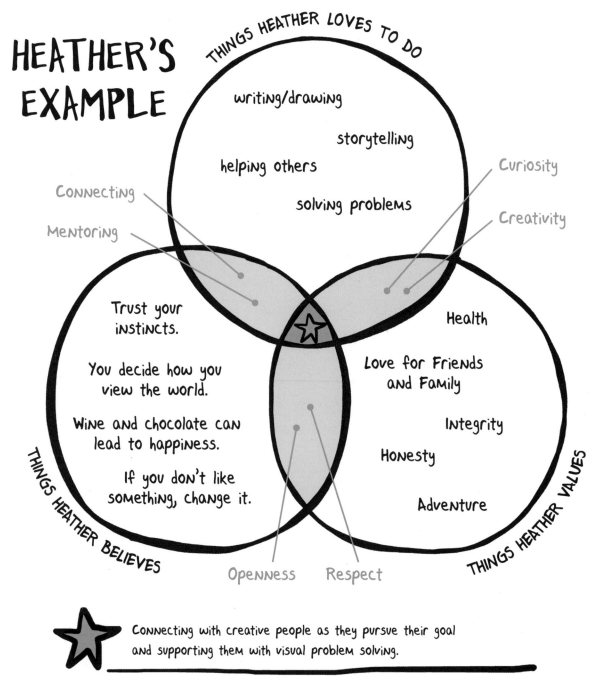

HEATHER'S EXAMPLE

THINGS HEATHER LOVES TO DO

writing/drawing

storytelling

helping others

solving problems

Curiosity

Creativity

Connecting

Mentoring

Trust your instincts.

You decide how you view the world.

Wine and chocolate can lead to happiness.

If you don't like something, change it.

Health

Love for Friends and Family

Integrity

Honesty

Adventure

THINGS HEATHER BELIEVES

THINGS HEATHER VALUES

Openness   Respect

Connecting with creative people as they pursue their goal and supporting them with visual problem solving.

HEATHER'S PURPOSE

Take some time to review your completed diagram and identify where there is overlap. Can you articulate the essence of this overlap in a single sentence? This is the first step toward identifying your purpose. A heads-up that this is not an easy task—so be easy on yourself! Revisit this spread as you continue to refine your endeavor.

THINGS YOU LOVE TO DO

THINGS YOU BELIEVE

THINGS YOU VALUE

YOUR PURPOSE

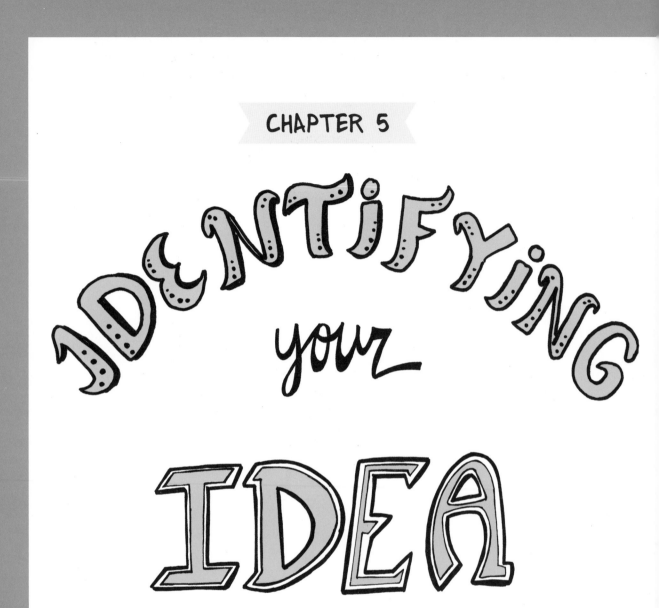

CHAPTER 5

IDENTIFYING your IDEA

You have passion and you have a purpose. Great. Now it's time to sketch out all of your ideas and assess them in relation to the world beyond. What problems do you see that need solutions? What do people need and what do they want? Imagine your idea, fully realized and out in the marketplace. Whom does it benefit? How does it generate revenue? Who are the paying customers? Are other people offering the same solution to the same problem? Answering these questions helps you identify your market. Before you act on your idea, you need to be able to clearly picture this market and your place in it.

Write all your . . . IDEAS

Choose your favorite idea and refine it
using the following exercises.

PROBLEM

A successful idea is more than a thought—it is a solution to a real need or problem. Identify a problem and its solution.

SOLUTION

With your idea in mind, consider who your competition might be. Who is their customer? What message are they sending to their customer? How is your idea different?

COMPETITOR

MESSAGE

CUSTOMER

How are you different?

ASSESSING the MARKET

Now that you have identified a few potential competitors, expand your thinking and consider the entire marketplace as it relates to what you will be creating. What comparable products or services are in excess in the marketplace? What is lacking?

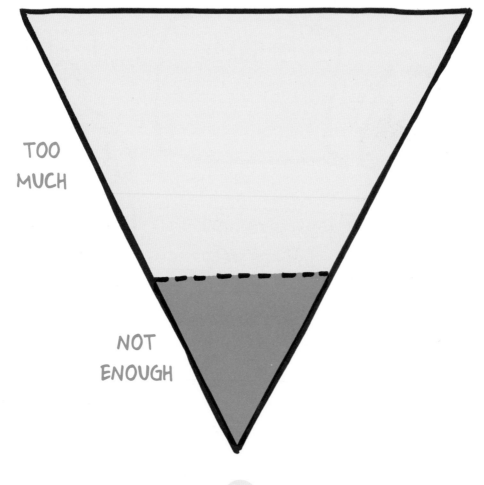

TOO MUCH

NOT ENOUGH

RUN YOUR
IDEA PAST
THE PEOPLE
YOU TRUST.

Record their
reactions here.

DESCRIBE YOUR IDEA Crystallized

You refined your idea in the previous exercises. Based on what you learned, draw or describe the new iteration of your idea.

WHAT DID YOU LEARN IN THIS CHAPTER?

How does your idea express your passion?

What problem does it solve in the world?

What about this is new or different from what already exists?

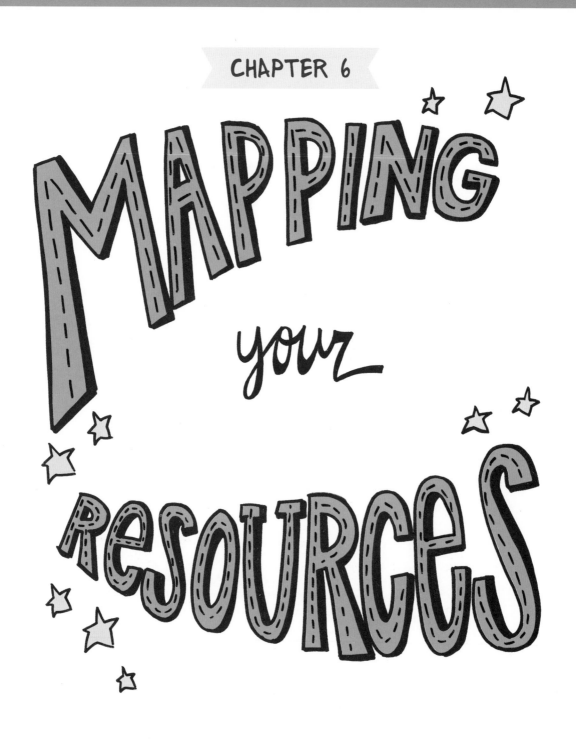

CHAPTER 6

MAPPING your RESOURCES

You can't do it alone. You will need support. The good news is that you already have a tremendous amount of resources in the form of people, places, and ideas. This section helps you take inventory of these resources.

Your network is a web of relationships. These connections can be established through a variety of commonalities and can have different dynamics and outcomes, resulting in a web that extends much farther than you realize. As you inventory all the resources you have and the fortuitous way they entered your life, remember that putting energy into finding people you can help is just as important as finding people who can help you.

FAVORITE
gizmos

MAP YOUR ENVIRONMENT

START LOCAL. Take a look around. What is in your neighborhood and community that can help you along the way? Which coffee shops are quiet and have good Wi-Fi? Which ones are more lively and have good pastries for coffee dates? What free services and classes are available near you? Does your neighborhood library have conference rooms or host meet-ups? The people who run all these locations, events, and activities are valuable resources. Get to know local business owners, community groups, and neighbors. On the next spread, map your environment. See Nora's example for inspiration.

A Great Place to Be

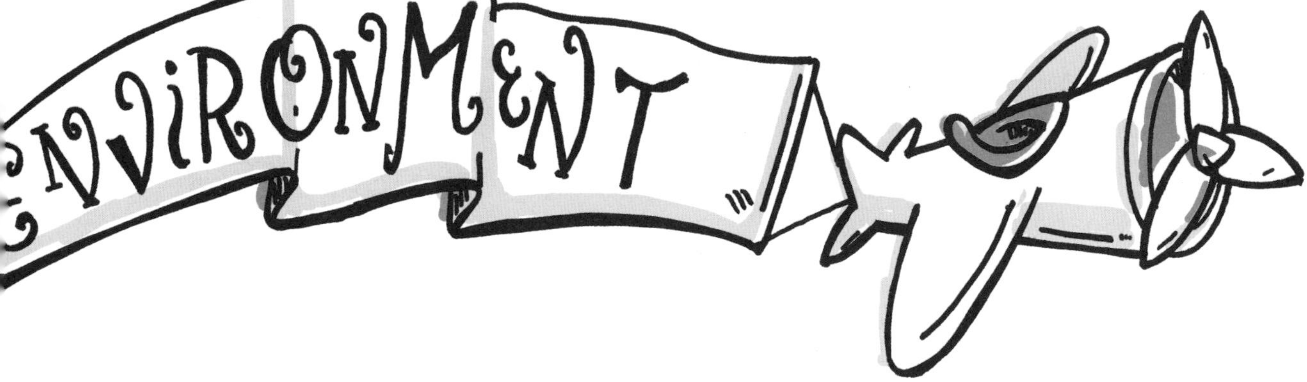
ENVIRONMENT

MAP YOUR NETWORK

A strong network can help you along the way. Fortunately, you already have many fantastic people in yours and it is larger than you think! Before you worry about making new connections, take a look at the ones you already have. On the opposite page, Heather mapped out her network, listing her contacts in various realms of her life.

Turn to the next spread and map out your own network in the space provided.

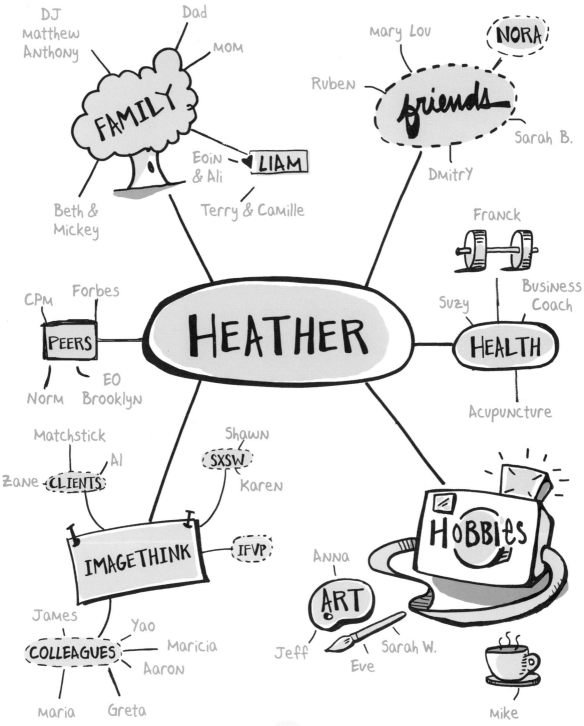

Put yourself in the center. Start with your current work situation. Make each person you know a spoke. List a few important characteristics about them, such as areas of expertise or hobbies. If you know people they know, list them as spokes and continue. Stop when you have created a wheel of amazing, informed, and well-connected people.

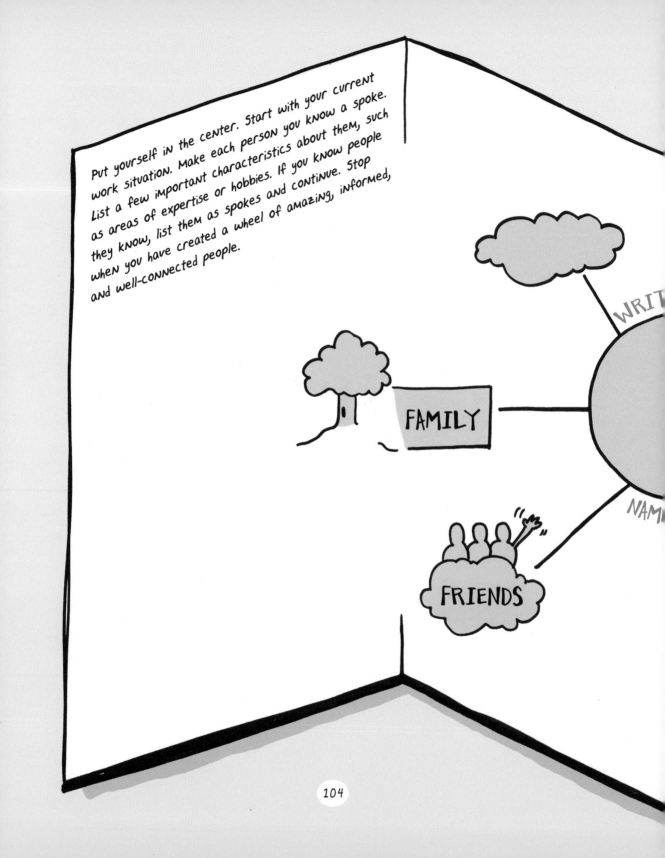

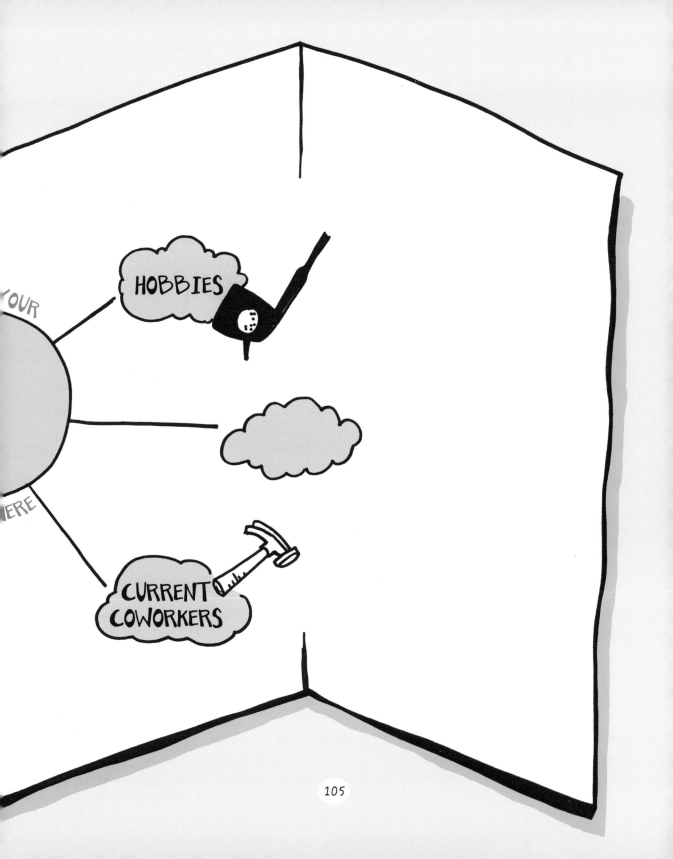

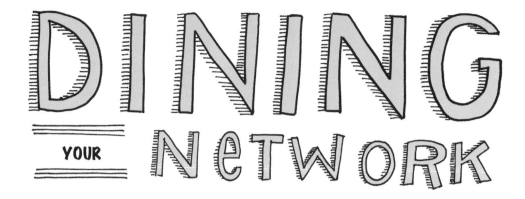

DINING YOUR NETWORK

Take a look at your network map. Identify three people you don't know very well who might be able to help you, teach you something, or who you are simply interested in getting to know. Call them. Yes, call them on the phone and ask them out for coffee.

Before you go, do a little research about them. Come prepared with questions and one thing you can offer them as well. A book you think they would enjoy, someone you can introduce them to.

Use the following pages to write down your questions and the insights gleaned.

MAKE THE DATE

PERSON · PLACE · DATE · TIME

COFFEE WITH _____.

QUESTIONS

INSIGHTS

DRAW YOUR FAN CLUB!

CHAPTER 7

PICTURING
your
CUSTOMER

In the previous chapter, you mapped your resources and established your network. Now look toward the future at the people who are going to be on the receiving end of your endeavor. Depending on the nature of your endeavor, they might be the consumer of your product, your advocate, or your client. For the purposes of this book, we will refer to them as your customer.

In this chapter we lead you through a process of identifying and empathizing with your ideal customer, which will help you decide how to focus your resources (in this case, time or money, or both) while also identifying the people, companies, or organizations that you aspire to work with. Speak to them and others will follow.

Get into your customers' heads and their hearts. What do they love? What challenges do they face that you might be able to help them with? Developing a complete picture will help you craft a message that will attract them.

WHO IS YOUR *Ideal* CUSTOMER?

Draw them.

Remember me? Tips on page 18.

WHO IS NOT YOUR Ideal CUSTOMER?

CIRCLE ALL THAT APPLY TO YOUR CUSTOMER

Identify where they might vacation, what they like to drink, how they like to spend their time, and what their favorite gizmos might be.

My CUSTOMERS

Where do they shop?

Where do they live?

What do they read?

A DAY IN THE LIFE

Imagine a day when your customer interacts with you. Walk in their shoes through that day, start to finish. Where are they going? What are they doing?

What will your customers love about your idea?

In this chapter, you became better acquainted with your customer. Now go a step closer by personalizing the essentials they keep in their back pocket.

CHAPTER 8

SHARING

your

MESSAGE

Now that you have outlined your ideal customer, how will you get the word out to them about your endeavor? The following exercises will help you arrive at clear, convincing, and memorable ways to talk about what you can offer the world.

We will ask you to consider how the form of communication impacts how your message is received and understood by your customer. We will also ask you to explore various marketing techniques—which will help you learn which one is best suited to your endeavor—and to consider how you can maximize your marketing resources.

IF YOUR ENDEAVOR WAS a ...

This fun exercise is common in branding workshops. Stretch yourself by writing or drawing answers to the following prompts. Next to each of your answers, write why you chose it.

PLANT

COLOR

ANIMAL

MOVIE

STYLE

FOOD

BOOK

DESIGN A CEREAL BOX

Imagine your endeavor is a tasty breakfast treat.

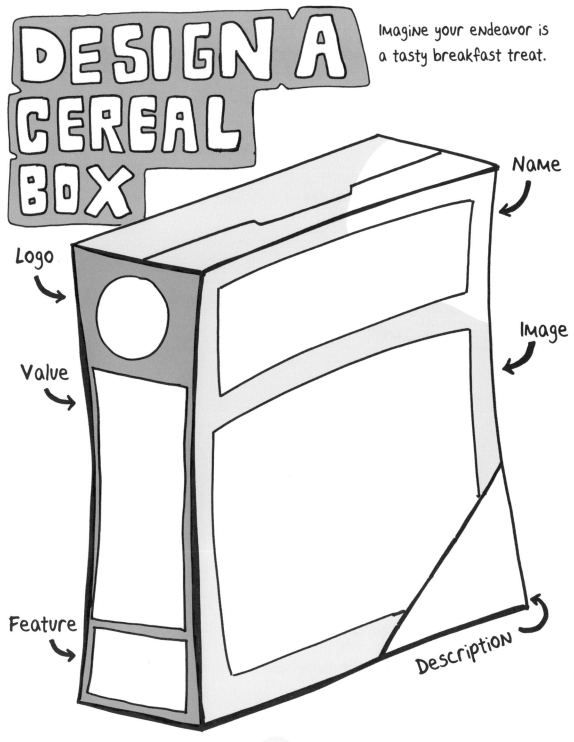

Name

Logo

Image

Value

Feature

Description

Imagine you are talking about your endeavor using different forms of communication. How do you reposition your message to suit each one?

Short and simple. Describe your business in 140 characters.

Don't be shy!
TWEET US
#DRAWYOURBIGIDEA

HOW YOUR CUSTOMERS find you...

WORD OF MOUTH

MEDIA

OTHER

WEBSITE

SOCIAL MEDIA

Fill out the pie chart to reflect how customers might discover your endeavor if you launched it using the resources that are available to you today.

HOW YOU WANT YOUR CUSTOMERS TO find YOU...

WORD OF MOUTH

MEDIA

OTHER

WEBSITE

SOCIAL MEDIA

Now fill out the pie chart to reflect how customers
might discover your endeavor if you had unlimited resources.
What can you do today to make this a reality?

Now imagine that the only resource you have is determination.
Use this space to brainstorm ways you can get the word out for free.

HOW DO YOU KNOW IT'S WORKING?

Marketing is the mad science of trial and error. When you are trying to see if your approach is working or not, consider indicators such as time, money, and what people are saying.

135

Cocktail talk

"So . . . what have you been up to?"
You know you will be asked. Work out your
answer below. Make it sweet and simple!

CHAPTER 9

DRAWING

your

SOLUTIONS

This chapter presents visual approaches to all types of situations you will encounter. You might have begun this book with a problem, or an unfulfilled wish. To find solutions or make things happen, you have to make decisions. Some of these decisions you can make when you're ready, whereas others have to be made swiftly and will force you to quickly find solutions.

Decision-making is the nexus of creativity. To be creative you have to make choices. This section helps you unpack your assumptions and reflect on small accomplishments and disappointments, which will guide you to uncovering solutions.

Feeling like you need eight
arms? Write down all the
different roles you play to make
your endeavor happen.
If you wouldn't hire
yourself for any of
those roles, don't!
Assign those roles
to someone else.

BREAK DOWN
your WALL

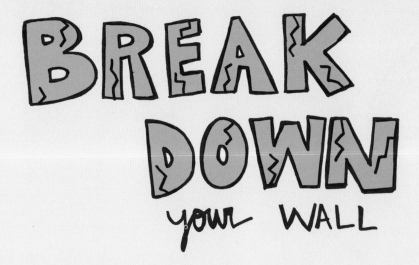

Hitting a wall—which can mean anything from running out of resources to temporarily burning out—can be discouraging. Persevering and breaking down that wall can reveal how much you really want something. Think of a wall you are approaching right now. What is it? What tools will you need to get through it?

STRUGGLING WITH A PROBLEM?
Take a look from a different perspective.

What does your problem look like from a distance? How far out into the world does this problem spread? Does it seem smaller from far away, or even bigger? Do you see new tools and resources that might be available to you?

Outcome

Experiment

Conclusion

Just like the artist's studio or the scientist's laboratory, the best ideas come from experimenting. What kind of experiments can you test on your idea? What are the results? What can you conclude from them?

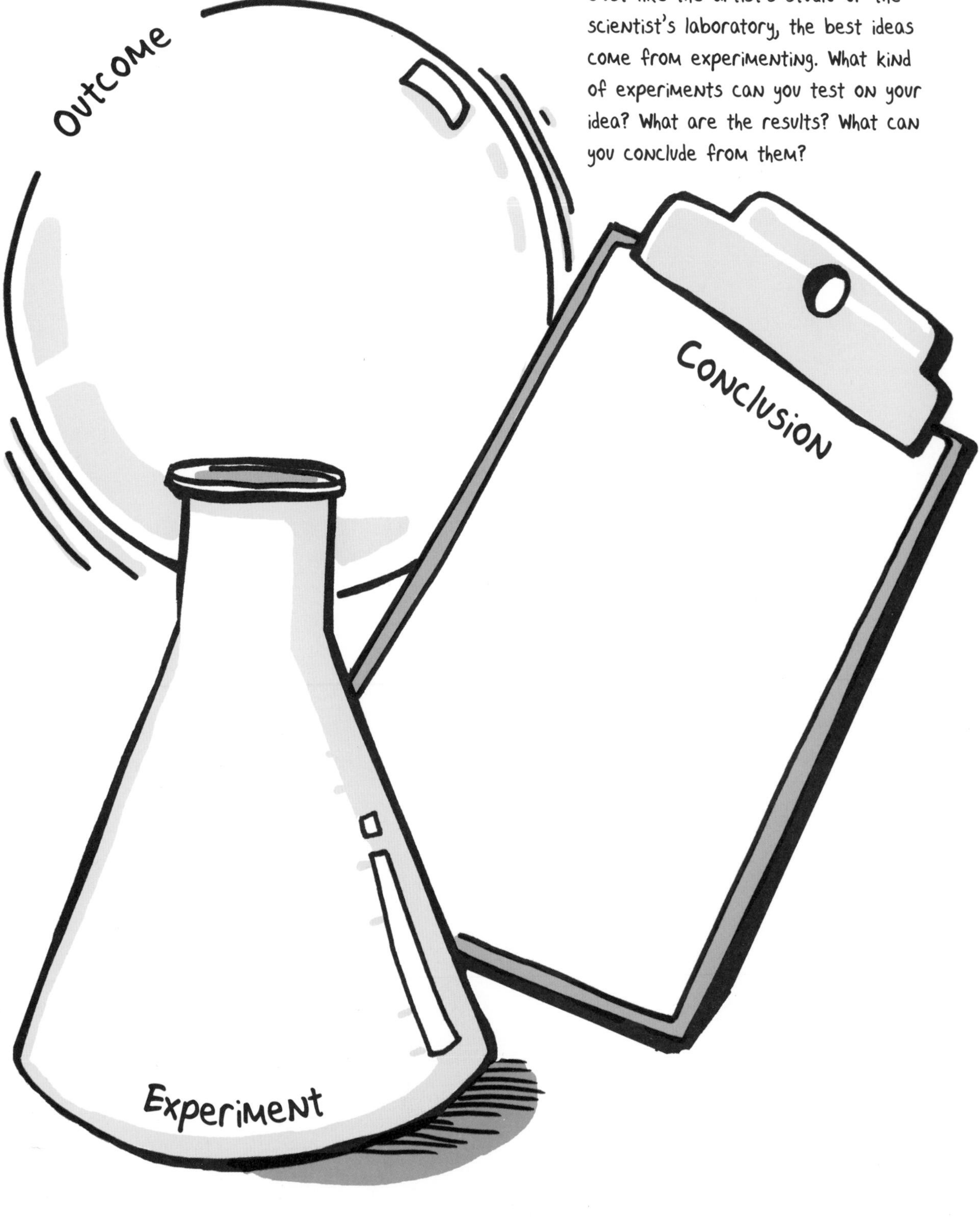

Well **THAT** didn't go very well . . .

What can you learn from your mistakes?

WHERE IS THE PONY?

We first heard the Pony Story when our business was in its infancy and we were building our website out of Heather's spare bedroom. It was so funny and useful that the punch line has become a phrase we continue to use regularly.

THE STORY GOES LIKE THIS:

It is Christmas morning at the house of two small boys who have very different temperaments. One boy finds a shiny new pocket watch in his stocking. Upon opening it, he begins to cry because he is immediately worried about breaking it. His brother discovers horse manure in his stocking. He runs to his father and shouts in excitement, "Daddy, Daddy, I got a pony! Now I just need to find him!"

Whenever we are faced with an annoying, disappointing, or truly upsetting problem, we ask each other where the pony might be.

Use the next page to list the horse manure in your situation and then reflect on the positive outcomes or circumstances that came with it. Where is the pony?

146

What would happen if you

DIDN'T DO IT ALL?

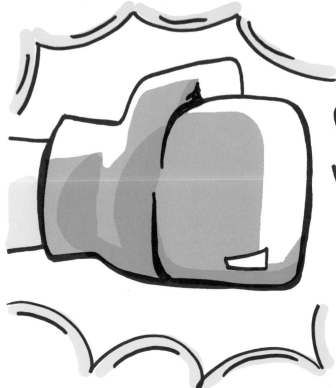

APPLY YOUR
STRENGTHS
TO A CURRENT PROBLEM

Refer back to the fears you listed on page 41. How do they show up in your pursuit? Which of your strengths can you employ to put them to rest?

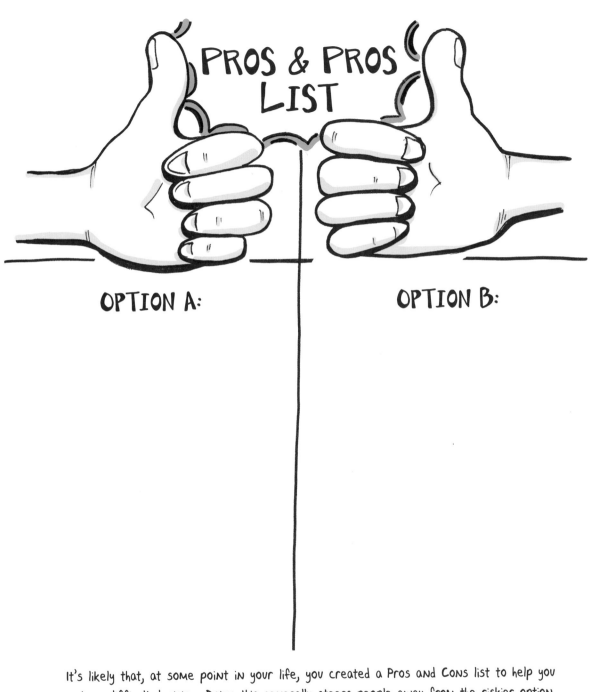

PROS & PROS LIST

OPTION A:

OPTION B:

It's likely that, at some point in your life, you created a Pros and Cons list to help you make a difficult decision. Doing this generally steers people away from the riskier option. However, sometimes the riskier option proves to be the better choice. On this Pros & Pros list, we ask you to imagine two choices you are faced with, but list only the benefits of both. Now, which scenario would you choose?

TIME TRACKER

Take stock of how you are spending your day by filling in this pie chart. For example, how much time each day are you currently spending on planning, networking, and researching? Consider all applicable activities and draw them as pie slices on the chart. How do you feel about the results?

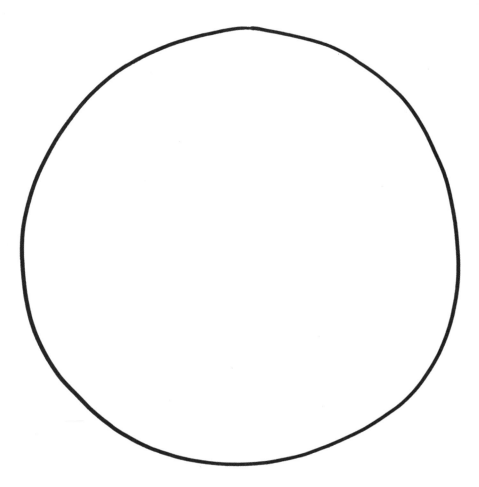

HOW would you Like it to Look?

Would you like the pie chart on the opposite page to look different? What would a pie chart reflecting your ideal day look like? Create it in the space below. Then consider what needs to change to make this ideal day a reality.

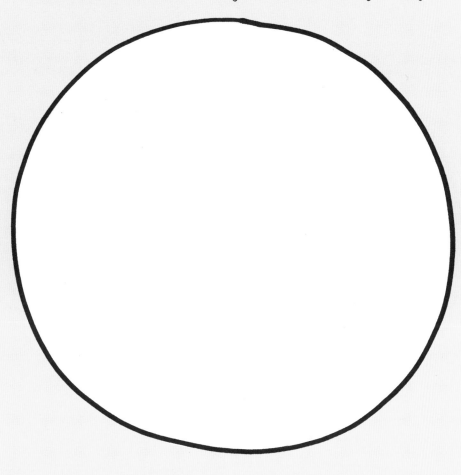

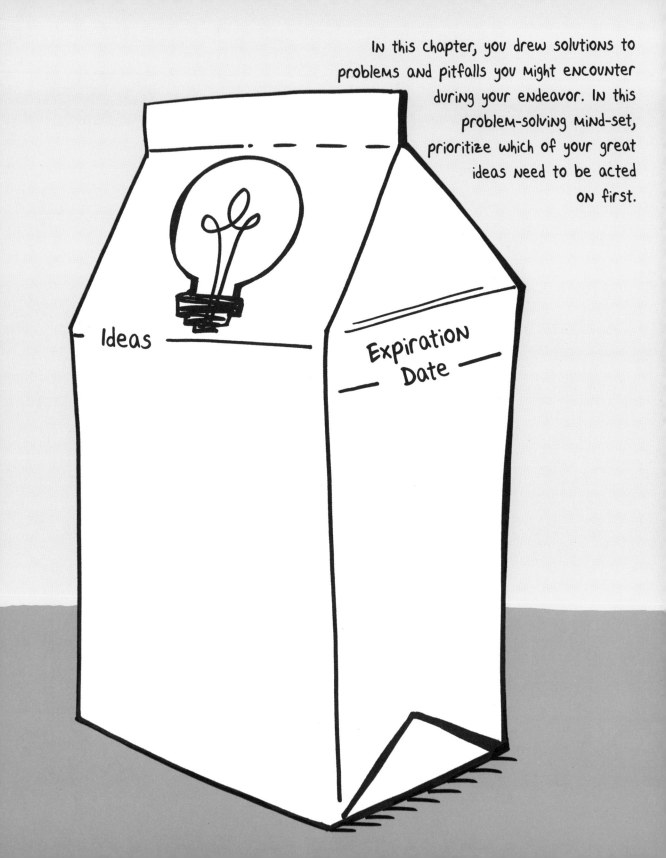

In this chapter, you drew solutions to problems and pitfalls you might encounter during your endeavor. In this problem-solving mind-set, prioritize which of your great ideas need to be acted on first.

Ideas

Expiration Date

CHAPTER 10

Charting your Path

When setting goals that will move you closer to actualizing your endeavor, it's important to clearly identify and articulate goals that are actionable and measurable. Aspirations like "being the best" or "delivering great service" aren't effective as goals because they are difficult to quantify, which means you can't be certain whether you have succeeded or failed. However, if your goal becomes "getting 90 percent 5-star reviews on Yelp" or "being featured in a major publication" you can truly measure your progress and pat yourself on the back when success happens.

The most effective way to make sure that you end up going where you want to go is to imagine yourself in the future. What does it look like? Now, work backward. What needs to happen now and along the way to ensure you get there?

This section contains several exercises for mapping your goals. Making your aspirations visible and charting a path to them is a powerful first step. You have gotten your journey underway by completing the previous chapters. This chapter will help you chart your path beyond this book . . .

Send yourself a postcard from your future self. Can't wait for you to be here!

WRITE OUT YOUR GOALS FOR 5 YEARS FROM NOW

WORKING

LEARNING

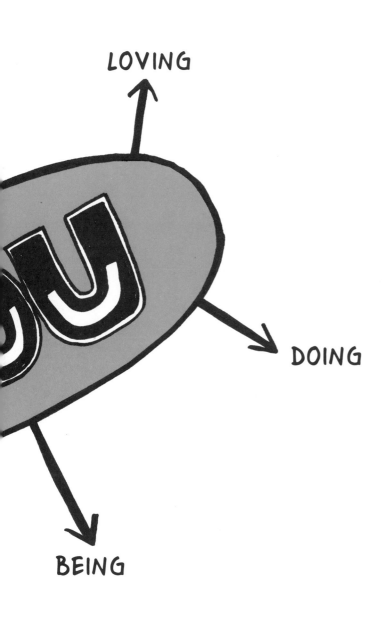

LOVING

DOING

BEING

WRITE DOWN YOUR GOALS FOR 12 MONTHS FROM NOW

WORKING

LEARNING

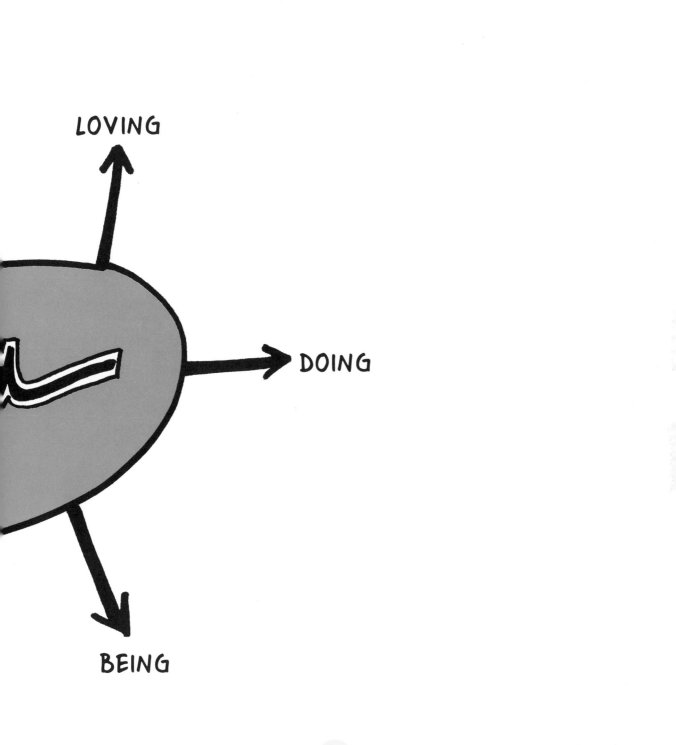

LOVING

DOING

BEING

Think of a goal you'd like to achieve in the next year. On this spread, describe your current situation, not having met the goal yet. Then consider your future situation after the goal has been met. What challenges and pitfalls might separate you from the future you envision? On the arch, write down what you need to do to bridge the gap.

PRESENT

CHALLENGES

charting a path

Now break down your goal from the previous exercise into the steps it will take to reach it. These are your milestones. Record them in the markers along the path. Then identify the strengths, skills, and resources you will gather as you travel the path. Write them down on the path to guide your way.

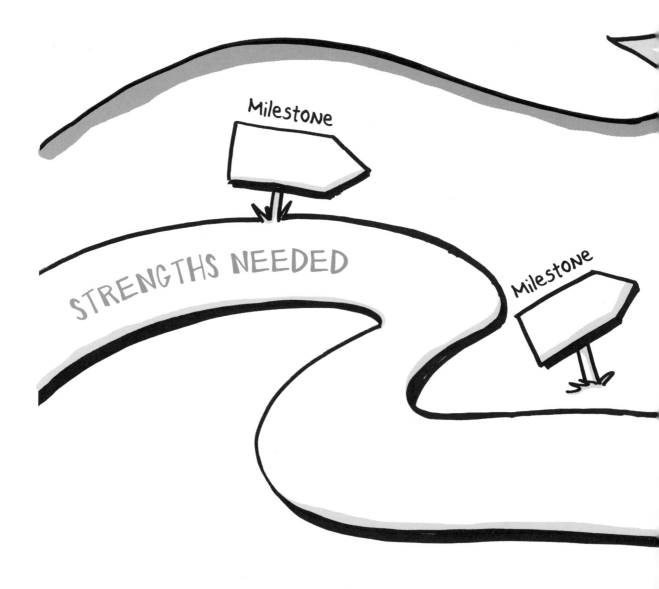

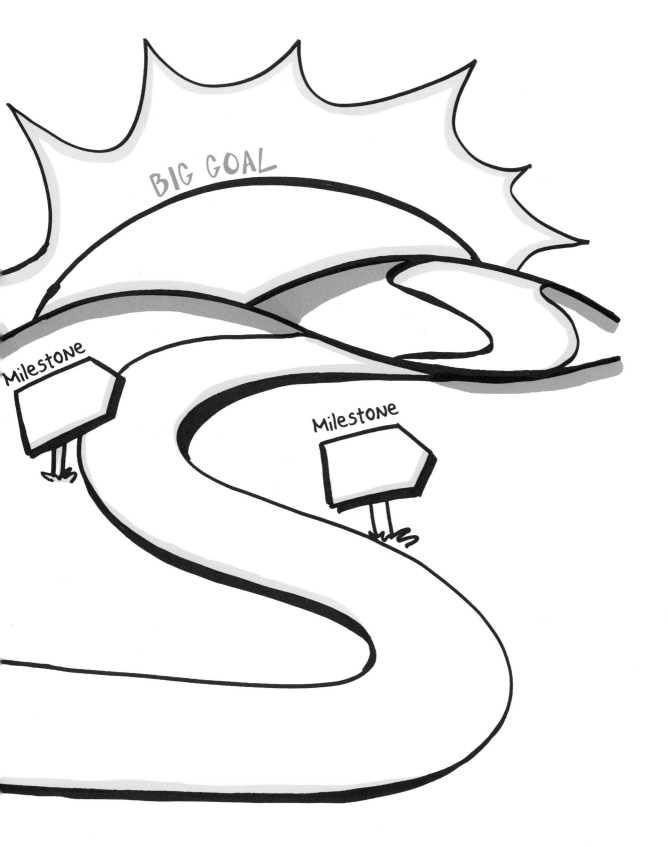

Celebrate SMALL VICTORIES

We never miss the chance to celebrate the big victories and we are less attentive to the small victories. But small victories deserve to be celebrated too! Use this spread however you like to celebrate having victoriously completed this book.

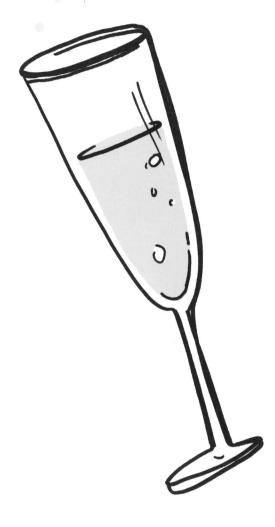

Congratulations, you did a lot of hard work here!

Reflect for a moment on what you've learned. You've identified what energizes you; you've put your passions into action; you've drawn out your purpose. As you look toward the future, your vision is crystal clear and your idea is solid as a rock! With your support network tucked in your back pocket, you are ready to share your message with your customers. You know them inside and out and can empathize with what they are thinking and feeling. Because you clearly know your purpose, you can speak to them with authenticity—and they want to engage with you! You can look at your endeavor and see the rewards in the risks, and tap into your strengths to overcome the threats. Knowing that you are taking action, you sleep better at night; and when you wake up rested, you pour milk in your coffee reminded of your key priorities for the day. Having charted your path, you are fully aware that there are sharks in the water, but you mapped milestones along the way and they motivate you to keep moving forward. And when you hit those milestones, you will let yourself celebrate the big (and little) successes.

Let's not fool ourselves—there will be bumps in the road. But when the going gets tough, you now have the resources to do a little problem solving. Remember that with the right tools and attitude, the pony is never too hard to find.

Congratulations for drawing out your big idea! We can't wait to see what you will create.

ImageThink is a graphic recording firm founded in New York City in 2009 by Nora Herting and Heather Willems. Featured in TED Talks, on the *Today Show*, and in *Forbes* and the *Wall Street Journal*, ImageThink has visualized the big ideas of some of the world's most influential thought leaders and companies, including Google, Pepsi, and NASA.

Cofounder NORA HERTING is a principal and graphic recorder at ImageThink and an award-winning artist with a background in education and facilitation. A former visiting professor at Denison University, Nora has taught courses in art and visual problem-solving and has served as an artist-in-residence at numerous institutions. She lives in Brooklyn, New York.

Cofounder HEATHER WILLEMS, also a principal and graphic recorder at ImageThink, is a business strategy consultant with a background in art and education. An advocate for entrepreneurial artists, she is a board member for EO Brooklyn, the Brooklyn branch of global network Entrepreneur's Organization. She lives in Brooklyn, New York.